Local Government Budgeting: A Guide for North Carolina Elected Officials

Julie M. Brenman
with Gregory S. Allison

UNC | SCHOOL OF GOVERNMENT

The School of Government at the University of North Carolina at Chapel Hill works to improve the lives of North Carolinians by engaging in practical scholarship that helps public officials and citizens understand and improve state and local government. Established in 1931 as the Institute of Government, the School provides educational, advisory, and research services for state and local governments. The School of Government is also home to a nationally ranked graduate program in public administration and specialized centers focused on information technology and environmental finance.

As the largest university-based local government training, advisory, and research organization in the United States, the School of Government offers up to 200 courses, webinars, and specialized conferences for more than 12,000 public officials each year. In addition, faculty members annually publish approximately fifty books, book chapters, bulletins, and other reference works related to state and local government. Each day that the General Assembly is in session, the School produces the *Daily Bulletin*, which reports on the day's activities for members of the legislature and others who need to follow the course of legislation.

The Master of Public Administration Program is a full-time, two-year program that serves up to sixty students annually. It consistently ranks among the best public administration graduate programs in the country, particularly in city management. With courses ranging from public policy analysis to ethics and management, the program educates leaders for local, state, and federal governments and nonprofit organizations.

Operating support for the School of Government's programs and activities comes from many sources, including state appropriations, local government membership dues, private contributions, publication sales, course fees, and service contracts. Visit sog.unc.edu or call 919.966.5381 for more information on the School's courses, publications, programs, and services.

Michael R. Smith, Dean
Thomas H. Thornburg, Senior Associate Dean
Frayda S. Bluestein, Associate Dean for Faculty Development
L. Ellen Bradley, Associate Dean for Programs and Marketing
Todd A. Nicolet, Associate Dean for Operations
Ann Cary Simpson, Associate Dean for Development
Bradley G. Volk, Associate Dean for Administration

FACULTY

Whitney Afonso
Gregory S. Allison
David N. Ammons
Ann M. Anderson
A. Fleming Bell, II
Maureen M. Berner
Mark F. Botts
Michael Crowell
Leisha DeHart-Davis
Shea Riggsbee Denning
James C. Drennan
Richard D. Ducker

Joseph S. Ferrell
Alyson A. Grine
Norma Houston
Cheryl Daniels Howell
Jeffrey A. Hughes
Willow S. Jacobson
Robert P. Joyce
Kenneth L. Joyner
Diane M. Juffras
Dona G. Lewandowski
Adam Lovelady
James M. Markham

Janet Mason
Christopher B. McLaughlin
Laurie L. Mesibov
Kara A. Millonzi
Jill D. Moore
Jonathan Q. Morgan
Ricardo S. Morse
C. Tyler Mulligan
David W. Owens
William C. Rivenbark
Dale J. Roenigk

John Rubin
Jessica Smith
Karl W. Smith
Carl W. Stenberg III
John B. Stephens
Charles Szypszak
Shannon H. Tufts
Vaughn Upshaw
Aimee N. Wall
Jeffrey B. Welty
Richard B. Whisnant

Printed in the United States of America

21 20 19 18 17   3 4 5 6 7

ISBN 978-1-56011-729-2

About the Series

Local Government Board Builders offers local elected leaders practical advice on how to effectively lead and govern. The booklets in this series provide topic overviews, specific tips on effective practice, and worksheets and reflection questions to help local elected leaders improve their work. The series focuses on common activities for local governing boards, such as selecting and appointing committees and advisory boards, planning for the future, making better decisions, improving board accountability, and effectively engaging stakeholders in public decisions.

Vaughn Mamlin Upshaw, lecturer in public administration and government at the UNC School of Government, is the series editor.

Other Books in the Series

Leading Your Governing Board: A Guide for Mayors and County Board Chairs, Vaughn Mamlin Upshaw, 2009

A Model Code of Ethics for North Carolina Local Elected Officials, A. Fleming Bell, II, 2010

Creating and Maintaining Effective Local Government Citizen Advisory Committees, Vaughn Mamlin Upshaw, 2010

Working with Nonprofit Organizations, Margaret Henderson, Lydian Altman, Suzanne Julian, Gordon P. Whitaker, and Eileen R. Youens, 2010

Public Outreach and Participation, John B. Stephens, Ricardo S. Morse, and Kelley T. O'Brien, 2011

Local Government Revenue Sources in North Carolina, Kara A. Millonzi, 2011

Getting the Right Fit: The Governing Board's Role in Hiring a Manager, Vaughn Mamlin Upshaw, John A. Rible IV, and Carl W. Stenberg, 2011

The Property Tax in North Carolina, Christopher B. McLaughlin, 2012

Suggested Rules of Procedure for the Board of County Commissioners, Joseph S. Ferrell, Third Edition 2002

Suggested Rules of Procedure for Small Local Government Boards, A. Fleming Bell, II, Second Edition 1998

Contents

Introduction

The adoption of a budget is one of the most important activities undertaken by local government officials each year. The budget serves as the elected board's primary opportunity to establish community priorities and to put its money where its mouth is. The budget also serves as a tool for planning community services and programs, communicating priorities, and properly managing finances. The budget process, however, with its big numbers, multiple acronyms, and counterintuitive rules, can be confusing. This guide is intended to remove the mystery of the budget process and to equip North Carolina's city and county governing bodies with the tools they need to actively participate in the process.

Many forces impact the budget, in particular, the state of the economy. Budget officials and members of local government boards must therefore consider economic forecasts for growth or decline in determining the budget. Federal and state governments often impose new mandates on local governments that also must be addressed. In addition, citizens increasingly want a greater say in the budget process and are no longer satisfied to wait until the next election cycle to offer input. Regional and national—sometimes global—cooperation and competition impact budgets. Changes in operations, circumstances, and legal requirements are constant, with technological advancements offering local governments the opportunity to streamline and advance their operations, but at a cost.

Although government revenues fluctuate in good economic times as well as in bad, most governments have entered into a period of protracted austerity, what many local officials view as the new normal. In the past, short-term budget cuts could be made to deal with cyclical economic downturns, but the trend has shifted toward more permanent reductions in support of governmental programs. Local governments are facing tough choices that will impact the quality of life in their communities for years to come.

Budget adoption is not an isolated, once-a-year agenda item for the board's consideration. Although budget *adoption* occurs as an annual event, the budget *process* is actually ongoing throughout the year, for both staff and elected officials. The implementation of budgeted activities as well as monitoring performance and spending, reviewing priorities, and making adjustments to the budget all occur on a cyclical basis.

Figure 1. Implementing the Budget

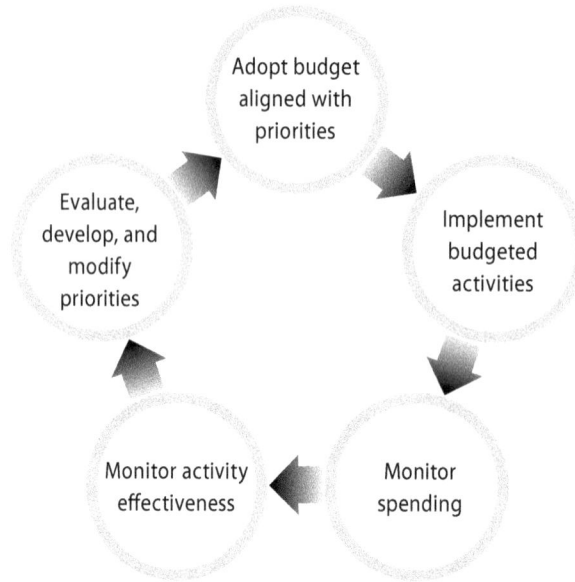

Adopt budget aligned with priorities → Implement budgeted activities → Monitor spending → Monitor activity effectiveness → Evaluate, develop, and modify priorities

As Figure 1 depicts, the task of implementing the budget begins as soon as it is adopted. Such decisions as whether new programs are to be put into practice or existing services are to be changed or eliminated are usually made during the budget adoption phase as part of the task of aligning the government's activities with its priorities. To ensure that accounts are not overspent, spending is monitored throughout the year through a framework for monitoring and accounting that is laid out in the budget. Also throughout the year, local government programs are monitored for effectiveness to help identify which are successful and which are not achieving the desired outcomes. Likewise, changing circumstances can lead to a change in priorities and revenue estimates, which in turn may require shifting budgeted resources and adopting mid-year amendments to the budget. The budget cycle thus operates continuously to ensure that local government resources are being allocated effectively.

Questions for Discussion

1. What goals do we have for our city or county budgeting process?
2. How well does our current budgeting process align with these goals?
3. What could our governing body and local government professionals do to budget more successfully?

Legal Requirements

The Local Government Budget and Fiscal Control Act (Article 3, Chapter 159, of the North Carolina General Statutes (hereinafter G.S.)) sets out a uniform system for the adoption, administration, and fiscal control of local government budgets in the state of North Carolina.[1] The most important legal requirements are summarized here and outlined in more detail in Appendix A. As defined in G.S. 159-7(b)(1), the budget is "a proposed plan for raising and spending money for specified programs, functions, activities or objectives during a fiscal year." State law requires each local government to have a budget officer and further specifies which government officials are to serve in that capacity. In communities with a city or county manager (manager form of government), the manager is the budget officer. In communities with other forms of government, other employees, including the mayor, may be appointed as budget officer. There are a few prohibitions against certain officials serving as budget officer in certain circumstances. For example, the sheriff may not be the budget officer for a county, and the register of deeds may not be the budget officer in a county with a population greater than seventy-five hundred. In larger communities, a separate budget office typically handles the duties of the budget officer under the direction of the city or county manager. In many communities the finance director handles the functions of the budget officer. In small communities, the manager or administrator often performs those duties.[2] Whatever the size of the staff involved in developing the budget, the process is similar.

By statute, the local government's budget must be adopted by the governing board in the form of a budget ordinance that "levies taxes and appropriates revenues" for a fiscal year.[3] The budget ordinance authorizes all financial transactions of the local government except for those authorized by a project ordinance and those accounted for in an

---

1. The Local Government Budget and Fiscal Control Act can be accessed at www.ncleg.net/EnactedLegislation/Statutes/HTML/ByArticle/Chapter_159/Article_3.html.
2. G.S. 159-9.
3. G.S. 159-7(b)(1).

intragovernmental service fund or a trust or an agency fund.[4] In North Carolina, local governments are required to adopt a balanced budget ordinance where "the sum of estimated net revenues and appropriated fund balances is equal to appropriations."[5] Revenues and appropriations are listed separately in the budget ordinance and must be exactly equal. A community cannot propose to spend more money than it anticipates receiving in revenue. However, a community can allocate funds from its reserves or fund balance[6] to offset revenue shortfalls. Similarly, a community can add to its reserves when possible.

All money received and expended by a local government should be included in the budget ordinance. No local government may expend any money, regardless of source, unless it accords with the budget ordinance or a project ordinance.[7] The budget can be amended during the year, however; the process and appropriate circumstances for amending the budget are described in later sections of this booklet.

As extensions of state government, North Carolina local governments may provide services or raise revenues only as explicitly authorized by the legislature. These authorizations are made by statute. Some communities are individually authorized to impose revenue or provide a service through local acts that apply only to designated communities. Clearly an important legal consideration in developing a budget is whether or not the community is authorized to impose a revenue or provide a service. The major revenue sources available to North Carolina cities and counties and the major services that cities and counties are authorized to provide are presented in Table 1 and Table 2, respectively, both presented in Appendix B of this booklet.

Questions for Discussion

1. Where do our city or county revenues come from?
2. What are cities able to spend their moneys on? Counties? What services does our city or county spend money on?
3. What information does our city or county's budget ordinance provide?

---

4. G.S. 159-7(b)(2).

5. G.S. 159-8(a).

6. *Fund balance* is a term used to describe the amount of money in a fund that is not planned to be spent—in other words, the amount of money that would be left in the bank for savings. Fund balance is described more thoroughly in the section titled "Key Financial Policies for the Budget."

7. G.S. 159-8(a).

The Budget as a Policy Tool

The budget serves as an annual statement of the policy priorities of the local government. Areas that receive significant funding have a greater priority than those to which fewer funds are allocated. The budget is thus the most powerful opportunity for elected officials to influence the programs and policies they want to see carried out in their communities.

While most budgets are adopted annually, and year-to-year changes tend to be incremental, they should not be created in isolation. Many governments have a variety of plans in place, ranging from strategic plans and comprehensive land use plans to capital improvement plans and department or area-specific plans. The recommendations of these plans should be taken into consideration when the budget is being developed. For instance, if economic development is the community's top priority in its strategic plan, the budget should reflect strategies that promote economic development. On a smaller scale, if a parks and recreation master plan indicates that the number one priority is the development of a new baseball field, funding should be allocated to the baseball field before a new soccer field is developed. Using these plans to guide the budget process is beneficial because most have already been adopted by the governing body and were developed by technical experts with stakeholder input. In other words, these plans have already been vetted, take into account community priorities, and have buy-in by elected officials.

How does this budget relate to future goals rather than just continue what we have done in the past?

The benefits of using adopted plans as a guide to establishing budget priorities will not be realized, however, if the various plans in place are disconnected from each other and were created without considering fiscal constraints or trade-offs between their conflicting priorities. For example, a facilities plan may prioritize the consolidation of government services within

What are the budgetary implications when considering a new plan, program, or policy? What is the cost of implementation?

an office park in order to save on building costs while a programmatic plan prioritizes providing service within neighborhoods in order to be close to users and an economic development plan prioritizes investment in downtown. A decision to adopt all three plans, despite their competing values and priorities, can lead to confusion when using the plans to guide budgeting decisions. In addition, even if a plan with numerous goals has been adopted, the budget is not required to fund implementation of the entire plan. This may upset some interest groups or local government staff who assumed that adoption of the plan made funding to fully implement the plan a done deal.

Planning processes are often lengthy. Some plans are initiated by one group of elected officials only to have an entirely different group receive the finished report. Other plans are long-range and take years or decades to fully implement. In addition, circumstances and priorities can change during the time it takes to proceed from initiation to adoption and finally to implementation. Elected officials need to recognize that they have a responsibility to serve as trustees of the public good, which sometimes means continuing work initiated by others but also sometimes means changing course based on an evolving political, social, demographic, or regulatory environment. Current elected officials are not bound by the decisions of their predecessors, but they need to take into account the impact of their choices and recognize that budget decisions should not be made in isolation. A choice to

To what extent is this budget consistent with our adopted plans and their priorities?

fund the aforementioned soccer field instead of the baseball field as a result of heavy lobbying by the soccer advocates may disenfranchise the members of the public—and perhaps the staff—who were involved in the development of the parks master plan. Yet, depending on the current financial circumstances and priorities of the community, it still may be the right decision to make.

Not all communities have previously adopted plans in place to guide budget development, and even those that do should revisit their priorities annually. In the absence of plans, annual goals that define funding priorities should be developed to guide the budget process. Elected officials should approve these priorities, and the staff should develop a budget that reflects the adopted priorities. As discussed in the next section, goals and priorities are often developed during board retreats.

Questions for Discussion

1. How are priorities set for our city or county budget?
2. What long-term plans have been adopted for our city or county?
3. How closely does our city or county budget follow a master plan?
4. How closely does our budget reflect annual goals?

Budget Development Process: The Board's Role

The primary purpose of budget development is to guide the policy direction of the city or county and enable elected officials to legally adopt the budget. Tough decisions have to be made in the budget process, and there will almost always be trade-offs. If, for example, the governing body needs additional resources in order to expand a program, it might call for a tax increase or a reduction in spending for another program. Much of the budget development process is a negotiation—between the budget officer and staff, between the board and the budget officer, and between the board and the public. By establishing clear priorities and using an inclusive, transparent process, the board's decision making can conclude with a budget that includes no surprises and is acceptable to everyone.

Board Retreats

The budget process should start with the end in mind: What is the board's vision for the community? What are the broad community goals that the board wants to achieve? What level of taxes and fees is appropriate for achieving these community goals? Many local governments begin each year with a special retreat where elected officials and key appointed managers set out this vision and goals. These retreats provide a useful framework for the process the staff will use in developing the budget. Even if a formal retreat is not held, it is useful for elected officials to provide guidance to staff early in the budget process to ensure that the budget is developed consistent with the elected officials' expectations. Some communities have found it helpful to have the governing body vote prior to the development of the budget on a set of guidelines covering key issues for the staff to consider. For instance, the guidelines may cover any permissible adjustments in the tax rate, new programs to be implemented, proposals regarding the hiring of new staff or the laying off of existing staff or decisions on whether or not reserves may be used to balance the budget.

Board retreats can be helpful beyond the budget process in helping develop a sense of teamwork among elected officials and staff, clarifying communication preferences, and

Budget Balancing Tactics

Local governments are always searching for ways to balance their budgets, whether in the midst of an economic downturn or simply to provide low-cost services to their communities. A survey of local governments identified the most commonly used budget balancing tactics. Whether a government cuts costs or raises revenues to balance the budget, all of the options have consequences that should be weighed before pursuing them.

Cost-Cutting Moves

Hiring freeze
Delay in capital improvements, maintenance
Across-the-board budget cuts
Cancellation of contracts
Contracting out
Energy- and water-saving tactics
Purchasing restrictions
Equipment cutbacks
Memberships in professional organizations
Travel restrictions
Training restrictions
Position cutbacks
Employees reassigned to other departments
Service cutbacks—hours of service
Support to outside groups
Revised staffing protocol
Four-day workweek
Furloughs
Reduction of work hours
Salaries/wages/compensation
Overtime
Reduced employee benefits
Health benefits
Intergovernmental collaboration/
    coordination—purchasing
Information technology remedies
Retirement incentives
Volunteerism
Work rules/policies
Modification of the budget process

Revenue-Enhancing Moves

Tax increase
New tax
Fee increases and expanded fee services
New fees
Reduction of fee subsidies
Tactics to increase receipt of existing taxes/fees
Cash management practices/investment strategies
Asset sales
Leasing of government assets to outside parties
New state/federal grants
Receipts from utilities
Drawing on reserve funds

Note: For more details on these tactics, see David N. Ammons and Trevor A. Fleck, *Budget-Balancing Tactics in Local Government* (Chapel Hill: UNC School of Government, Feb. 2010), http://sogpubs.unc.edu//electronicversions/pdfs/BudgetBalancing.pdf?.

spending an extended period of time in a more informal setting to build camaraderie. Some communities have the retreat led by the mayor or board chair, the manager or administrator, or a skilled human resources employee. Many communities prefer to hire an outside facilitator so that all participants may contribute without having to take on the role of retreat leader. A skilled facilitator plays a neutral role, thus allowing all participants to voice their opinions, and can help retreat participants stay on task and achieve goals in an efficient and inclusive environment.

In order to provide a more relaxed atmosphere, retreats typically are held in a location outside of normal government meeting rooms. The cost of room rental, particularly if the retreat is held in a resort-type location outside of the community, should be weighed carefully so as to avoid the appearance of excess. It is important also to follow public meeting laws and provide appropriate notice of the retreat as well as public and press access to the retreat as observers. While the presence of the public and the press can diminish the unrestrained conversation that is often strived for in retreats, the need for open government prevails. The press, in particular, can be a valuable partner in sharing the government's priorities with the public.

Budget Hearings

While a retreat is often the beginning of the budget process, a budget hearing often comes at the conclusion of the budget process. After the budget officer has presented the budget to the board, they often will hold a series of work sessions on the budget. The budget officer or department directors will present detailed budget information to the board, and the board in turn will ask for more detailed information about the level of services that will be provided for in the budget. Because a public hearing is required after the board receives the budget, but prior to their final vote, the board will have an opportunity to listen to feedback from constituents on the contents of the budget. Some of this public comment will be sharply critical.

Many board members focus specifically on tax and fee levels proposed in the budget, whereas others use the opportunity to more broadly discuss governmental operations, praising their favorite services and critiquing those they feel are less essential. During these budget hearings, the board may identify areas where they want to change the proposed budget, but since board members usually have different opinions on what is important, there is almost always a need to compromise on the contents of the final budget. After the board has provided its feedback, the budget officer will revise the budget accordingly and bring it back to the board for a final vote.

Questions for Discussion

1. How does the governing body provide guidance to professional staff in advance of the budgeting process?

2. How does the governing body set priorities for the city or county?

3. How does the governing body convey its goals and priorities to the administration?

Budget Development Process: The Staff's Role

Once the staff has received preliminary direction from the elected officials, the staff budget development process begins. The Government Finance Officers Association (GFOA) is a valuable resource for local government budgeting professionals. Appendix C summarizes the twelve elements of the budget developed by the GFOA, which outlines the various recommended phases of a budget process.

Budget Calendar

The staff should develop a budget calendar in consultation with the elected officials. The calendar should include such dates as

- the board planning or budget retreat,
- the staff budget kickoff,
- deadlines for departmental budget submissions to the budget officer,
- staff training on budget systems or requirements,
- opportunities for public input,
- when the budget officer will present the proposed budget to the board,
- board meetings when the budget is expected to be discussed and voted on.

A number of budget deadlines are dictated by state law. The budget calendar must take these dates into consideration. Specifically:

- The fiscal year begins July 1 and ends June 30.[1]
- Before April 30 of each fiscal year, each department head is to transmit budget requests to the budget officer.[2]

---

1. G.S. 159-8(b).
2. G.S. 159-10.

- The budget, along with a budget message, is to be submitted to the governing board not later than June 1.[3]
- Before it adopts the budget ordinance, the board must hold a public hearing.[4]
- Not earlier than ten days after the day the budget is presented to the board, and not later than July 1, the governing board must adopt a budget ordinance.[5]

Budget Kickoff

The budget officer will want to kick off the budget cycle process each year. The kickoff may be in the form of a memo to city staff participating in the budget process, a meeting of department directors, or a larger meeting incorporating all staff levels. The kickoff should include information about the key deadlines, including the budget calendar; the form in which the budget should be submitted; and what approach to the budget the administration will be taking. It is appropriate to use the kickoff to set the tone for the budget season. For example, is the government anticipating major program reductions and layoffs, or will there be opportunities for developing new services and program expansions? Should departments prepare a budget for the status quo to minimize change or propose reorganizations to achieve service delivery efficiencies or cost savings?

In the budget kickoff, staff should be informed how the budget will be tackled. The financial and political climates weigh into this determination. Choices about the level of specificity required for budget requests and the manner in which requests should be made should be described at this time. Expectations for the level of involvement in the budget process also should be defined. Some communities use a top-down approach whereby executives make decisions about the budget with little involvement from other staff. Other communities actively seek employee input through suggestion boxes and open forums or by providing incentives for identifying money-saving initiatives. While North Carolina law does not recognize collective bargaining or public employee unions, it may be beneficial to reach out to employee groups for their input. Keeping employees informed about what budget trade-offs are being considered can be an effective management tool, and allowing for two-way communication between employees and management can only strengthen the organization.

---

3. G.S. 159-11(b).
4. G.S. 159-12(b).
5. G.S. 159-13(a).

Sample Budget Calendar

Month	Activity
January	• Board Retreat—set priorities. • Staff budget kickoff; department directors begin to prepare budget requests.
February	• Community meetings held to solicit public input on budget.
March–April	• Departmental budget requests submitted to budget officer. • Staff compiles all budget requests.
May	• Budget officer presents budget to the board.
June	• Board work sessions held on budget. • Public hearing held on budget. • Budget ordinance must be adopted by June 30. • Prior fiscal year ends June 30.
July	• Fiscal year begins July 1; budget becomes control instrument for all expenditures.
August–October	• Annual audit or comprehensive annual financial report on prior year's expenditures is completed and presented to the board no later than October 31.
November	• Management team begins discussing goals for next fiscal year.
December	• Staff begins preparing budget guidelines; trains staff on use of budgeting software.
Ongoing	• Monitoring of revenues and expenditures occurs throughout the year. • Budget amendments may be processed throughout the year.

Many communities find it useful to develop a budget manual that contains a compilation of the information relayed in the budget kickoff, including instructions for submitting budget requests and additional information about the budget process. Also included in the budget manual would be information about the computer systems being used to compile the budget. Up-front information on any hot-button issues about particular types of expenses or programs should be included as well so that the staff can anticipate questions that will be asked about these issues. For instance, the use of travel funds, consultants, new vehicles, or overtime pay might require extra justification. By anticipating questions from the board or the community, the budget officer will be better prepared to defend the budget when it is publicly debated.

Typically the kickoff and the budget development process is a staff-oriented process. Elected officials should provide guidance prior to the budget kickoff to help set the tone, and it is appropriate for them to receive updates on decisions and trade-offs that the administration is making. However, the development of the nuts and bolts of the budget process is generally a staff responsibility.

Whether a budget director, finance director, city or county manager, or someone else, the budget officer will usually project revenues available to the community and identify priority areas for investment and opportunities for savings or enhanced revenues. The methods used for calculating revenues should be carefully considered as they impact the total amount of funds available for the government's budget. The budget officer will work with each department to develop a budget for that department and then compile the various requests into a unified budget. It is very useful at this stage to already have the board's budget guidelines so that when decisions are being made about what to include and exclude from the budget—before the board has ever seen it—they are made in a manner consistent with the board's priorities.

The budget officer will present a proposed balanced budget to the board, together with a budget message, no later than June 1. Typically the budget officer is the primary point of contact with the board regarding the contents of the budget and, together with department directors, answers questions from the board about the details of the budget proposal during budget deliberations.

Departmental Budget Requests

A typical budget development process would be for each department to prepare a budget request to submit to the budget officer. The departmental requests usually include the cost for maintaining current services as well as suggestions for expansions or contractions of services. This is often the first stage where decisions will be made about what services will be included and excluded from the budget request. A departmental budget request made in an environment of unlimited resources will look very different from one made in an environment of serious financial constraints. Departments may take into consideration any or all of the following in prioritizing their budget request:

- the cost of maintaining existing services;
- resident demand for expanding or constricting service;
- new laws or court settlements that require additional services or changes in the way services are provided;
- previously adopted strategic or business plans that laid out priorities or timelines;
- changes to the way of doing business that will allow for more efficiency or better service;
- trends in their field that need to be addressed;
- current performance standards and whether or not the department is meeting expectations;
- facility needs, including expansion, maintenance, and accessibility; and
- changing costs of supplies and contracts.

Has your department proposed any cost-saving efficiencies in the budget? In what ways will these changes impact service delivery?

Department directors should have the best sense of the priorities for their respective departments and also should be able to identify opportunities for expense savings as well as potential revenue enhancements.

It is good to keep in mind that, for several reasons, current services may cost more in the next fiscal year. For one, salary and benefits for employees may increase, as might operating costs, such as fuel, electricity, or rent. A program or service that began in the middle of one fiscal year may need funding for an entire twelve-month period in the next fiscal year. In addition, a multi-year contract approved this fiscal year may require increased costs or scope in subsequent years. On the other side, some costs may decline or be eliminated, such as equipment purchases.

As noted above, after departmental budgets are submitted to the budget officer, they are all compiled into a single budget for consideration and approval.

Case Study: Departmental Revenues

The budget officer often takes the lead in projecting all organizational revenues, but some departments will also be involved in projecting revenues for their particular services.

Election Revenues. The total cost of elections is shared by the county elections department and the municipalities that are holding elections during the fiscal year. The elections department will determine how many voting sites will be open and what portion of each ballot will be attributed to the municipalities holding elections. The elections department will estimate the revenue it will receive from each municipality for the election.

Development Revenues. Plan review and building inspection revenues are dependent on the amount of construction and site plans that occur in the community each fiscal year. Planning department staff usually are able to anticipate the number of projects coming forward in the community and estimate their revenues based on the current economic environment, historical trends, and fee levels.

Water Revenues. A water utility will use trends in water sales to anticipate revenues for the water system. If a major industrial user is expanding its operations, sales will increase. An environmental campaign to conserve water, conversely, may reduce sales. A rate structure may be proposed that makes water more affordable for low use but more costly for high use. All of these factors, along with historical trends in water consumption, will impact the projected water revenue for the fiscal year.

Recreation Fees. Some recreation services, such as access to a public park, are provided free of charge, while others are provided on a fee-for-service basis. A fee schedule is typically set outlining the cost to participate in various programs, such as entrance to the swimming pool, participation in a youth athletic league, or enrollment in an art class. Many communities offer reduced fees for low-income participants or a higher fee for non-resident participants. Revenues are calculated by estimating the number of participants (typically based on historical trends) and the fee charged per participant.

Questions for Discussion

1. How does the governing body learn about department budgets?
2. What level of input does the governing body expect to provide staff regarding the budget preparation process?
3. What trade-offs do board members think are okay? Off limits?
4. How does the governing body use information about department budgets?
5. How does the governing body help department heads manage budgets successfully?
6. How is budget information presented to the governing board?
7. Who should board members turn to for budget information? The manager/administrator? Department directors? Finance/budget staff?

Budget Development Process: The Role of Other Participants

Government Employees

Many governments do not involve the majority of their employees in the budget development process unless it is directly a part of their job duties. Even though employees are directly impacted by many of the decisions in the budget, ranging from pay and benefit packages to staffing levels and program enhancements or reductions, they often only find out what is included through news reports. Some governments find it useful to proactively present budget updates to staff and solicit input from them. While local government unions are not recognized in North Carolina, there are often other employee associations that speak for groups of employees in an organized manner. Public safety officers may affiliate with an organization, such as the Police Benevolent Association or the International Brotherhood of Fire Fighters; administrative assistants may meet regularly to discuss implementation of work policy changes and be used as a liaison between management and other employees; and some governments help facilitate discussions of representative groups of employees throughout the year to improve communication. All of these types of employee groups can be used to enhance communication and elicit feedback about budget issues.

Budget Requests from Other Groups

A variety of other groups will make budget requests or advocate for programs of interest to them. Such groups will range in influence and authority, and the budget process should take into consideration how their input will be heard and whether their requests will be presented initially to the board or to the budget officer. Among these groups are

- residents and neighborhood associations;
- sports leagues, environmental clubs, or affordable housing advocates;

- nonprofits seeking grant funding;[1]
- business groups, such as the chamber of commerce;
- private sector firms that manage certain governmental functions, such as public facility management, janitorial services, security, parking services, and economic development;
- appointed advisory boards and commissions (e.g., planning commission, bike and pedestrian commission, recreation advisory committee);
- statutory boards, such as for social services and mental and public health services;
- other elected officials, such as the sheriff or the register of deeds;
- other governmental agencies, including school systems and the courts.

Do we have a process set up for hearing budget requests from people or entities outside of our governmental organization?

While municipal and county governments are both subject to budget requests, counties have a unique obligation in that their boards must approve funding for other elected officials and other entities over whom they have limited or no managerial control. In spite of this limited control, county boards are required to appropriate funds for these entities. This intergovernmental interaction brings up another important element of the budget development process, intergovernmental cooperation.

Intergovernmental Cooperation

All local government budgets are influenced to varying degrees by the situations of other governments. Problems such as the lack of transportation or affordable housing are regional issues and cross political boundaries. What one community does will impact another community. Joint cooperation between municipalities and counties in maintaining and operating such necessary countywide operations as the 911 emergency system is a practical necessity. Many issues require working across governmental boundaries to develop effective and efficient solutions. Joint agreements between governments for services such as public

---

1. More detailed information on government–nonprofit relationships can be found in Margaret Henderson, Lydian Altman, Suzanne Julian, Gordon P. Whitaker, and Eileen R. Youens, *Working with Nonprofit Organizations* (Chapel Hill: UNC School of Government, 2010).

transportation, mental health, and economic development have successfully saved money or provided improved service delivery in many regions of the state.

The state and federal governments provide various levels of funding to local governments. In addition to funding, the state and federal governments issue many laws and regulations that govern how and what the local governments can do with these funds. Health and human services budgets typically have more state and federal funds than local funds, and, consequently, these departments are required to carry out specific programs following prescribed protocol. Local governments tend to welcome state and federal funds, but it is important to recognize that this funding typically comes with strings attached, perhaps requiring local matching funds or changes in the way the local government operates. Federal and state funds are rarely flexible and can only be used for

What is our local government required to do in return for receipt of these funds? Do we need to allocate matching funds? Can we supplant existing funds?

specific purposes. Sometimes federal or state agencies issue rules or regulations that will be costly to implement. These mandates require local governments to change their operations despite not having been appropriated the funding to do so.

Some funding comes to local governments in the form of grants, whether from other governments or private sources. Grant funding typically is for a specific purpose and often for a time period that does not perfectly match the local government's fiscal year. Grant appropriations are not required to be included in the annual budget ordinance and frequently are set apart through a separate grant project ordinance. Once a grant project ordinance is adopted, it does not need to be re-adopted annually but, rather, is in effect until the grant funds are fully expended.

Are there any requirements after the grant has ended? Do we have the capacity to meet the reporting requirements of the grant?

The Role of the Citizen

Inasmuch as local government budgets are developed to provide services to residents and visitors of a community, it is appropriate that citizens have a say in the development of the local government budget. The exact form and frequency that citizens may utilize can vary greatly. The only legally required opportunity for citizen input is a public hearing on the budget prior to its final adoption. Citizens can provide input on their own, or the government can reach out to them for their opinions. Examples of opportunities for citizen input in the budget process include[2]

- voting for governing board members who then are entrusted to enact a budget reflective of their priorities;
- attending the single public hearing held prior to the final adoption of the budget;
- attending a public hearing soliciting comments on the budget prior to the development of board priorities;
- sending letters, emails, and phone calls to governing board members;
- writing letters to the editor of the local paper, commenting on articles on news websites or blogs and Facebook or Twitter posts about the government and its budget;
- responding to surveys of a randomly selected sample of the citizenry on their budget priorities;
- responding to feedback solicited by the government in a newspaper ad, Web survey, water bill insert, or resident newsletter;
- attending community meetings held at recreation centers, schools, or churches where board members and staff are able to hear from the community in a more informal setting;
- working with a like-minded interest group to coordinate support for its initiatives;
- attending a community budget workshop where a broad range of citizens discuss their priorities and gain a better understanding of competing priorities and values;
- providing input on specialized plans that the governing board can take into consideration when prioritizing funding in those functional areas;
- requesting services from the government throughout the year and thereby demonstrating demand for a particular service that can be taken into account in the budget process.

In addition, members of appointed advisory boards may be given a special opportunity for comment on budget priorities.[3]

---

2. For more information about citizen participation in government, including methods and reasons for citizen engagement, see John B. Stephens, Ricardo S. Morse, and Kelley T. O'Brien, *Public Outreach and Participation* (Chapel Hill: UNC School of Government, 2010).

3. For more information on working effectively with advisory boards, see Vaughn Mamlin Upshaw, *Creating and Maintaining Effective Local Government Citizen Advisory Committees* (Chapel Hill: UNC School of Government, 2010).

Soliciting public input on the budget has both positive and negative aspects. Members of the public often have narrow interests and do not always weigh the needs of the entire community when making their case. Citizens are typically not budget professionals and may not recognize the implications of their requests or understand the actual cost of a budget item. Also, it is time consuming and sometimes costly to engage citizens early on in the budget process.

On the other hand, carefully collecting citizen input can help the government understand the changing needs of the community. It can help justify program contractions or expansions. By affording citizens an opportunity to comment on the budget early in the process, the government can avoid the impression of holding the legally mandated public hearing without intending to make any changes to the budget because it is so late in the process. And of course the more citizens are able to participate as partners in the budget development process, the greater the citizen ownership of the final product.

The Press and Social Media

Both the press and social media can help local governments solicit public input. The reach of television news, newspapers, and blogs is often far greater than that of government newsletters, and though the traditional news media is usually interested in major local government budget decisions, coverage is often limited. It is therefore a good idea for the local government to be proactive and send out budget information to the media in an effort to encourage them to share this information with the public. The decisions made in the budget process are often complicated and hard to condense into a brief news report, so it is worth the effort to brief local reporters and answer all of their questions.

Traditional news coverage is increasingly being replaced by social media, ranging from websites and blogs to Facebook and Twitter. Local governments should consider sharing budget information via the Internet to reach out to more of their constituents.

Questions for Discussion

1. To what extent are local government employees involved in budget development?
2. What do you want to hear from staff? Citizens? Advisory boards? How does their input contribute to the budget process?
3. How much of our local government budget comes from state and federal sources?

4. How much of our local government budget is committed to intergovernmental activities?

5. Why is it important for our city or county to involve the public in the budgeting process?

6. How does the public currently provide input into your budget?

7. How might the city or county do a better job of obtaining or responding to public input? Would you like to see more or less public input?

8. What forms of public input have you used in your community? At what point in the budget cycle should they be used? Are there approaches you might want to use going forward? If so, which ones and why?

9. How can our community use the media and social networks to share information about our budget?

Budget Preparation, Contents, and Presentation

Just as there are different methods of preparing the budget, there are different methods of presenting and adopting the budget. State law allows the budget to be prepared in any manner that suits the local government so long as appropriations are made by department, function, or project and revenues are presented by major source.[1]

Budget Formats

Budgets may be assembled in a variety of formats. The format itself influences the way decisions will be made. The most common formats are the line item budget, performance budget, program budget, and zero-based budget (see the Common Budget Formats chart, p. 26). Some formats focus more on inputs into the budget, whereas others focus more on outputs or outcomes. Some require a level of accounting sophistication and effort that is hard to achieve with limited staff resources. Others require extensive citizen input to help prioritize and determine what the government can afford while others focus more on the well-being of the community. In addition, there are numerous variations on these standard approaches, such as budgeting for results, outcome budgeting, and price of government budgeting. Each format has pros and cons, all of which should be considered before the government opts for one or the other.

No matter which method is used in the development and presentation of the budget, the government chooses the level of detail to be used in the adoption of the budget ordinance. At a minimum, the major sources of revenues must be included in the ordinance. Smaller revenues may be grouped into categories. Likewise, appropriations must be made by department (e.g., police), function (e.g., public safety), or project. Additional detail may be included in the budget ordinance but is not required. A benefit of providing additional detail is that the budget lines will have been approved, meaning there will be less

---

1. G.S. 159-13(a).

Common Budget Formats

Budget Type	Description	Pros	Cons	Example
Line Item Budget	Most common form of budgeting. Presents a list of revenues and a list of expenditures separated into categories.	• Provides the most detail about what will go into the budget. • Provides the most control over how the money will be spent. • Easy to monitor throughout the year.	• Provides less flexibility for adjustments during the year. • Not focused on outcomes.	Cost of salaries for the budgeted number of police officers.
Performance Budget	Shows cost of providing certain levels of service and what outputs will be achieved.	• Focuses on the quantitative result that will be achieved rather than the individual line items that will be used. • Promotes efficiency because attention is focused on the cost per unit of service provided. • Provides departments with more discretion in what money is spent on.	• Less control over how the money is spent to achieve the outputs. • Sometimes hard to measure the outputs.	Instead of simply looking at the cost of police officers, this budget can focus on the amount spent per arrest made.
Program Budget	Shows cost of providing certain programs as a package and results in terms of outcomes achieved.	• Allows more flexibility to use the total expenditures for a program purpose rather than being tied to type of expenditure. • Typically uses a line item budget as its basis but breaks expenditures and revenues up into programs designed to accomplish a certain goal.	• Less control over what the money is spent on to achieve results. • Sometimes hard to measure outcomes.	A program outcome may focus on the percent of crimes solved.
Zero-Based Budget	Starts from scratch each year rather than using last year's funding as starting point for next year's incremental change in funding. This method breaks the budget up into a number of decision units, showing the results that will be achieved at various funding levels for each unit.	• The budget is presented in a way that provides information to decision makers about what will be achieved at the different funding levels. • The focus is on ranking options and explicitly choosing the level of service desired. • May be more responsive to changes in technology or social changes.	• Zero-based budgeting is time-intensive and requires thorough activity-based cost information in order to accurately develop the various scenarios.	The budget may offer a choice between a package that anticipates police responding within 5 minutes of service request and one where the response time would be 15 minutes.

opportunity for confusion later in the year. Conversely, additional detail can also lessen the local government's flexibility to move funds as the need arises during the year due to changing circumstances.

Biennial Budgeting and Multi-Year Projections

Some governments create biennial budgets for planning purposes. Proponents of a biennial budget believe it allows for improved management, financial reporting, and long-range planning, and it is true that compared to the more prevalent annual budget, the biennial budget provides more predictability in the government's operating expenses from year to year. Typically, a biennial budget provides a two-year spending plan for the government, but in North Carolina the budget is still required to be adopted annually. This means that spending during the first year is limited to that which was planned for the year and that revisions to the budget can be made before the second year budget of the two-year cycle is adopted.

While only a few governments formally adopt biennial budgets, many governments do prepare multi-year budget projections. These projections estimate the amount of revenue and expenses the government will have in future years, typically for the next five to ten years. Using historical trends, estimated inflation factors, known adjustments to contracts or debt schedules, reductions in one-time sources of funds or expenses, the maintenance schedule of capital assets, and planned programmatic changes, the budget office will make assumptions about the future revenues and expenses. These multi-year projections help governing boards and managers look to the future and identify potential structural problems with the budget. For instance, if the government has relied heavily on one-time revenues to balance the budget in the current year, a budget gap may be predicted for the next year.

Capital Budgets

Capital planning is essential for each community's economic development and strategic plan. Capital expenses, such as buildings, infrastructure, technology, and major equipment, are costly and usually need to be planned and paid for in a manner distinct from ongoing expenses. Just as individuals pay for groceries

How do proposed capital projects support local priorities?

and utility bills without the same planning and saving required to purchase a car or a house, local governments find it useful to prepare and adopt a capital budget separate from the annual operating budget.

Many local governments prepare a separate Capital Improvement Plan (CIP) that anticipates future capital needs. Because of the high cost of capital investments, part of the planning is to space out the various investments over multiple years to ensure that there are not large spikes in annual budgets. Multi-year capital plans identify and prioritize needs, establish project scope and costs, and estimate ongoing operating and maintenance costs.

Capital outlays may be paid for in a variety of ways. Options include

- paying with cash each year (sometimes called pay as you go);
- grant funding from federal, state, or private sector sources;
- saving money over multiple years in a capital reserve fund until enough is saved for the project;
- a bank loan where the principal and interest is repaid incrementally;
- general obligation bonds, which require voter approval and also are repaid incrementally;
- revenue bonds, which require the project to be able to generate sufficient revenue to retire the debt systematically;
- certificates of participation, another form of borrowing in which a separate legal entity owns the project and the government repays the debt in installments;
- tax increment financing where the incremental increase in tax revenues that will occur in a specified area due to the construction of the project will be used to retire the debt.

Cash is the lowest-cost method of paying for capital projects because there are no borrowing costs. The decision on how much to borrow and with which method is multifaceted. There are legal limits on how much each community can borrow as well as limits on what amount is prudent to borrow. Often a government will set a cap on the amount of debt it will tolerate, which usually is expressed as a percentage of the total budget. Many communities find that a combination of paying with cash and borrowing is the best method of smoothing out the peaks and valleys of capital spending.

What percentage of the budget is devoted to debt service? How does our city or county's debt compare to similar jurisdictions?

The government often adopts a *capital project ordinance* for each project. Unlike the budget ordinance,

the capital project ordinance does not need to be adopted each year but lasts for the duration of the project. This allows for longer term planning of projects that may take multiple years to execute. The annual budget will include funds for capital projects, even if separate capital project ordinances are adopted. Any annual allotments of cash for capital projects will be appropriated in the annual budget, as will debt repayments (formally called debt service) for any borrowing that has occurred. It is important to keep in mind that once a project is completed, ongoing maintenance and operating costs will need to be budgeted for annually.

Using Performance Measures in Budgeting

Data on the number and quality of government services can be collected and used to monitor government performance. Performance measures are useful in setting goals for government services, tracking progress over time, and comparing one government's performance with that of its peers. While budgets can be developed without performance measures, they typically are more robust when such data are used. Performance measures allow governments to monitor their impact on important community issues, such as the incidence of crime, the cost per ton to dispose of solid waste, or the percentage of persons in workforce development programs who become employed within three months of completion of the program. By coupling measures of the outputs, efficiency, effectiveness and outcomes of programs with the funding that is appropriated for them, budget creators can make better decisions about allocating funds.

Performance measures in some service areas are easier to develop than others. For example, monitoring response times to 911 calls is now routine for most public safety departments and is a measure of their efficiency. On the other hand, while a county health department can report on the number of low–birth weight babies born, it is more difficult to determine if the services the health department provided to pregnant women made an impact on that number because so many other factors can influence birth weight. While performance measures are valuable tools to help understand the effectiveness and efficiency of government services, care should be exercised in developing and using these measures to ensure that the services are being fairly judged.

How are our programs performing compared to our own goals? How are they performing compared to peer programs?

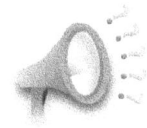

Case Study: Performance Measures

Streets. The city council had a high level of frustration with the condition of the roads in their city. The public works department requested additional funds to address the problem, but the city council blamed lazy workers and poor management for the excessive potholes and structural failures in the streets. No matter how hard the crews worked and how many procedural efficiencies they implemented, the city council was not satisfied with the results. The public works staff continued to work hard but also decided that some objective performance measures would help make their case. They were able to show that while the number of miles of road in the city increased, the street maintenance staff had decreased due to budget cuts, and they benchmarked the spending per mile of road with peer communities and demonstrated that their city was investing significantly less in street maintenance. Finally, they compared the length of re-pavement cycles in their city to industry standards in peer communities. While most communities repave their streets every fifteen to twenty years, this city was waiting fifty or more years to repave most streets. Through the use of performance measures, the city council recognized that the streets were in poor condition not because of lazy employees, but because of a lack of investment in the streets. As a result, the city was able to reprioritize its funding and dedicate more funds for street maintenance.

Economic Development. The county had long boasted that it owned its water plant and landfill free and clear. When meeting with prospective businesses, the commissioners touted low tax and utility rates as a reason to locate in the county and attributed the low rates to being debt free. Over the past year, the county had lost three large, industrial businesses to a neighboring county with higher tax rates. This was a big loss, as the businesses would have contributed significantly to the tax base and brought many jobs. The board asked the county manager to determine what could have been done differently to win the businesses. The businesses told the manager that they were concerned the county was not investing in maintenance of its water plant or planning for expanded capacity at the landfill. The manager proposed a more balanced set of measurements that addressed infrastructure maintenance and capacity in addition to debt load and tax rates. By monitoring a broader range of measures, the county would more comprehensively meet the community's economic development goals.

It is always smart to ask where in the budget you can find a piece of information you are interested in.

Budget Document

The format can vary from community to community, but most budget documents are presented in multiple sections. A budget may be presented as a single spreadsheet that summarizes revenues and expenses, breaking them down into a few categories. At the other extreme, a budget may be a large volume of several hundred pages with multiple sections, spreadsheets, and narratives. It can be overwhelming to review the budget, especially the first time.

Sample Contents of a Budget Document

Topic	Contents
Letter of Transmittal	• Summarizes the major issues and changes addressed in the budget.
Priorities	• Community vision, mission, goals. • Organizational chart. • Major initiatives to be funded with budget. • Linkage to strategic plan. • Performance measures.
Financial Policies	• Description of policies that impact the development, management, and monitoring of the budget.
Fund Summaries	• The general fund is the main operating fund of a government and is required. Most communities have multiple funds, such as enterprise funds, fiduciary funds, special revenue funds, or internal service funds.
Multi-Year Projections	• Typically the budget will integrate the current financial status with the outlook over the next several years to develop a longer ranging projection of the community's financial condition.
Departmental Budgets	• A summary of each governmental department's budget is presented. Often there is a narrative, a spreadsheet, and key performance measures to describe each departmental budget. The departments are often grouped into functions, such as administration or public safety.
Debt Management	• Describes the level of debt the community has incurred and how that debt is being managed.
Capital Projects	• While many communities have a separate capital improvement plan, a summary of the plan is often included in the annual budget.
Grant Projects	• Communities often receive grants to help finance their operations. The grants would be summarized here.
Community Profile	• Budget documents often include information about the community, such as population, demographics, major employers, and other information of interest.

A transmittal letter should accompany budget documents from the budget officer. The transmittal letter should highlight the most significant changes in the budget and how the community's needs are being addressed. A well-written transmittal letter will summarize the budget, leaving the reader with a good understanding of such concerns as changes to taxes and fees, programs that will be delivered, and the impact on staffing.

Most budget documents also include summary spreadsheets about the total budget as well as some information about each government department and the specific changes proposed to the departmental budgets.

GFOA Award

The Government Finance Officers Association (GFOA) operates the Distinguished Budget Presentation Award Program (see www.gfoa.org). Governments that receive this award are recognized for their preparation of the highest quality budget documents that reflect adoption of both the guidelines established by the National Advisory Council on State and Local Budgeting and the GFOA's best practices on budgeting. To receive the award, a government has to publish a budget that meets GFOA's program categories as a policy document, operations guide, financial plan, and communication device. Three independent evaluators review the submitted budget documents across twenty-seven categories. Budgets must be rated as proficient in fourteen mandatory categories to receive the award. The Distinguished Budget Presentation Award is one way a government can demonstrate its high standards in the budgeting arena.[2]

Questions for Discussion

1. What type of budgeting does our local government use? What works? What could be improved?
2. Does our city or county use performance measures? If so, what are they?
3. How does our city or county's budget compare to similar local governments?
4. How much of our budget changes annually?
5. What is our debt level? What is our debt tolerance? How is our debt level affecting our city or county's ability to accomplish long-term goals?

---

2. During Fiscal Year 2011, forty-nine North Carolina local government entities received the GFOA Distinguished Budget Presentation Award. Thirteen of those entities have received it for more than twenty years.

Key Financial Policies for the Budget

Governments need financial policies in place in order to govern how changes to the budget are made. Any change that is outside of the ordinance must be approved by the governing body through a budget amendment. Other changes to the budget, however, may be made with the approval of the budget officer. A threshold may be created dictating who is allowed to approve certain changes and what changes may be permissible in certain categories of expenditures but not in others. For instance, shifting funds between operating line items for utilities and office supplies may be permissible, whereas a shift from operating costs into salaries, or vice versa, may be prohibited.

Mid-Year Adjustments and Amendments

A local government may not spend money that has not been appropriated in the budget ordinance. If during the course of the fiscal year unbudgeted revenues come in, the money cannot be spent because it is not budgeted. Likewise, if unexpected expenses arise, money cannot be spent if it is not already budgeted. An amendment to the budget must be made to authorize both revenues and appropriations as part of the budget before the funds may be spent. Because the budget was originally adopted as an ordinance, a change to the budget requires a change to the ordinance, which is done via a vote of local elected officials.

As an example, if a community had budgeted $1 million in property tax revenues but receipts showed that actual revenues for the fiscal year would be $1.25 million, the seemingly extra $250,000 cannot be spent without an amendment to the budget ordinance in which the $250,000 is budgeted as a revenue source and, similarly, the $250,000 is budgeted as an appropriation. Budget amendments for a given fiscal year must occur prior to the end of the fiscal year (June 30). If during the audit of the fiscal year it is determined that spending exceeded the authorized budget, the board cannot retroactively appropriate additional funds.

As previously noted, the budget ordinance can be in any form that the board considers most efficient for decision making, but it must outline appropriations by department, function, or project and show revenues by major source.[1] Some governments adopt a very detailed budget, with each line item spelled out in the ordinance. Others summarize the budget details and appropriate lump sums for each department or project, or group departments together in categories, such as administration or public safety.

The amount of detail in the budget ordinance affects the level of flexibility the local government will have in making adjustments to the budget during the year. If the ordinance is detailed at the line item level, any adjustments to those line items require an amendment to the budget, which necessitates a vote of the board. A budget that is more summarized provides greater flexibility for the administration of the budget during the year without having to return to the board for a vote. Thus, while a more detailed budget gives elected officials more control over any changes to the budget, it also means that the government is more constrained in its ability to respond to changing needs, as all changes, big or small, need to be approved by the board. Regardless, it should be noted that any increase or decrease in an overall fund's budget requires formal board approval.

The board may amend the budget at any time, or, as noted above, modifications may be made administratively within the constraints of the ordinance that was adopted. The property tax rate, however, cannot be increased mid-year (unless ordered by the North Carolina Local Government Commission or a court). While budget modifications can be made at any time, it is important to note that there are costs associated with each change; the board may therefore want to limit the number of changes it makes to significant or time-sensitive ones. Budget changes that significantly alter policies or priorities should be carefully weighed. In some communities, amendments to the budget receive much more scrutiny than the budget itself. In others, the amendments are passed with little attention. Amendments to the budget are as important as the original budget and should be treated with the same care as the budget itself.

Carryovers

For a variety of reasons, some budgeted funds may not be fully spent during a fiscal year. The majority of unspent funds will be declared as surplus and revert to the fund balance. Some unspent funds, however, will be carried over from one fiscal year to the next. These funds may be for a contract that has been let but not completed, for a project that got a late start, or for a bill that was submitted late. Typically referred to as *carryovers*, these funds

---

1. G.S. 159-13(a).

need to be re-appropriated in the subsequent budget in order to move the budget authority from one year to the next. As the dollar amount of carryovers is typically not known when the budget is passed, the re-appropriation usually happens in the form of a budget amendment to the subsequent year's budget.

Fund Balance

Some money is budgeted each year without a specific plan for spending it. This *fund balance* represents the financial resources of the government on hand and often is referred to as the government's savings. It is a critical part of managing the cash flow of the entity. As revenue intake and expenditure outflow are not always evenly matched (especially because the largest source of revenue, property tax payments, are due in early January), it is important to have an adequate amount of cash on hand to meet monthly obligations. A local government's fund balance is to be used in emergencies when large unanticipated expenses occur. Fund balance is also often used as a financing alternative for planned or unexpected capital projects.

   Prior to expending the fund balance, the board is required to adopt a budget ordinance authorizing its use. Most governments have a financial policy specifying a target amount (usually a percentage of the total budget) that should be set aside as the fund balance. The state Local Government Commission requires the fund balance to be a minimum of 8 percent of the budget, and most communities find a higher target to be prudent. There also may be a correlation between keeping an appropriate fund balance level and a community's bond rating.

Contingency Budget

Some governments budget for contingencies or unanticipated expenses during the year. Unlike the fund balance, a contingency is specifically appropriated in the budget ordinance and can be spent during the fiscal year without an amendment to the budget. Typically the amount budgeted in a contingency account is small. North Carolina law limits contingency appropriations to 5 percent of the total fund amount.[2] Many elected officials believe that most budgets contain a cushion of "hidden money" that staff can access during the year.

Is there any "hidden money" in the budget? Does the budget include reserves for emergencies?

---

2. G.S. 150-13(b)(3).

Why Can't We Spend All of Our Fund Balance?

Fund balance represents the financial equity of a governmental fund. However, there are legal and practical limitations on the availability of fund balance at any point in time. Some view fund balance as simply representing the amount of resources in savings or in a slush fund to be used for whatever the governing body would like. It is certainly not that simple—fund balance has many components and forms. In generally accepted accounting principles, there are five potential classifications of fund balance. Specifically, they are nonspendable, restricted, committed, assigned, and unassigned amounts.

A quick description of each of these follows:

Nonspendable—The portion of fund balance that is physically not in a spendable form. The most common example is inventory.

Restricted—Resources in fund balance that are controlled by outside parties or laws. Elected officials may not change restrictions. The most common example of restricted fund balance would be grants.

Committed—The amount of fund balance that elected officials have dedicated for a particular purpose through an official action. Unlike restrictions, commitments are not legally binding and, thus, they can be changed but only through an official action.

Assigned—Portion of fund balance that *either* the elected official *or* the appointed manager intends to use for a particular purpose. However, no formal action has taken place, or more importantly, no formal action is necessary to change the purpose.

Unassigned—Amount of fund balance after all restrictions, commitments, and assignments have been identified. If this is a positive amount in the General Fund, for example, the resource is not restricted or identified for a particular planned use.

Contingency accounts avoid this impression and specifically set aside money for unexpected needs during the year. While contingency accounts are useful to address relatively small, unanticipated expenses, it is difficult to budget for an undefined, unanticipated expense when there are so many specific competing needs. Financial policies are useful to set parameters for how and under what circumstances the contingency funds may be accessed.

Questions for Discussion

1. How may the governing body modify its budget ordinance?
2. What policies does our governing board follow when making budget changes?
3. What guidelines does the governing board have for fund balance, contingencies, and carryover?

Monitoring the Budget

The adopted budget sets the framework for the accounting of a local government's spending throughout the year. The categories of revenues and expenditures and the dollar amounts in each category set limits on what can be done within the organization. As each dollar comes into or goes out of the government's accounts, it is recorded and tracked against what was budgeted in that category.

Reporting on the Budget

Throughout the year, the board should receive reports on the budget. These reports can serve as an important management tool for the elected officials as well as the administrators. Financial reports are often prepared monthly or quarterly. Usually reports are not prepared until the month or a quarter has *closed*, that is, after all the relevant transactions have been posted in the books. This can range from a few days after the end of the month or quarter to as many as forty-five to sixty days later, though shorter periods are recommended.

Boards should expect to see a report that at a minimum includes year-to-date revenues and spending compared to budgeted revenues and spending. Keep in mind that the flow of money in and out of the government's accounts is rarely spread evenly throughout the year, so it will not be unusual to see some large expenses incurred at the beginning of the year before revenues are collected later in the fiscal year.

It is also useful if the administration reports on the progress of major initiatives throughout the year. If a new fee schedule is to be implemented, new staff are to be hired, or changes are to be made to a program structure created as part of the budget, the board will want to receive periodic updates on the status of those initiatives. By using a uniform reporting tool, all board

If we are projecting lower than anticipated revenues, what are we doing to curb expenses as well?

members, as well as members of the public, will be able to monitor the implementation of changes proposed in the budget.

Questions for Discussion

1. What reports are available to monitor the budget throughout the year?
2. How do this year's spending rates compare to last year's?
3. Are we on track to end the year with a balanced budget?
4. How do we monitor the implementation of new initiatives?

Conclusion

The local government budget is a tool for managing a local government's finances, priorities, and services. It provides a vehicle for elected officials to move their agenda forward and become knowledgeable about an organization. While it is an imperfect, long, and very public procedure—and one that never completely satisfies everyone's interests—the budget development process nonetheless provides a great opportunity for local government officials to work with a broad range of people, effect improvements in operations, and make a positive difference in their communities.

WORKSHEET: *Checking Your Understanding of the Budget*

_____ The budget presents a summary of major revenue sources and expenditures.

_____ I understand where the local government's revenues are coming from and what factors most affect them.

_____ I understand how this year's budget differs from prior years' budgets.

_____ I am satisfied that this year's budget protects my community's financial future and meets today's most pressing needs.

_____ The budget describes long-term strategic goals for our local government.

_____ The budget addresses short-term changes in the government or community that have influenced decisions in the development of the budget.

_____ The budget articulates priorities and issues for the upcoming year.

_____ I know the role of the governing board and the role of staff during the budget process.

_____ I know how citizens, employees, and other interested parties can have a say in developing the budget.

_____ I understand the major legal requirements and constraints of the budget process.

_____ I know the budget calendar and when different activities will happen.

_____ I know how to ask smart questions about budget development and monitoring.

_____ The budget identifies fund balance.

_____ The budget includes information on current debt obligations.

_____ I understand how the budget can be changed mid-year and when it is appropriate to make changes.

_____ I know where to get the information I need to make informed budget decisions.

Note: This checklist, adapted in part from the GFOA *Detailed Criteria Location Guide for the Distinguished Budget Presentation Awards Program* (www.gfoa.org), can be useful for all communities when reviewing their budgets, whether they intend to apply for the awards program or not.

Appendix A:
Key Legal Requirements and Terms

A *budget* is a proposed plan for raising and spending money for specified programs, functions, activities or objectives during a fiscal year.

The *budget ordinance* is the ordinance that levies taxes and appropriates revenues for specified purposes, functions, activities, or objectives during a fiscal year.

- Each government must operate under a *balanced budget ordinance* where the sum of estimated net revenues and appropriated fund balances is equal to appropriations.
- All money received and expended should be included in the budget ordinance. *No money may be spent unless it is in accordance with the budget ordinance or a project ordinance.*
- Amendments to the budget ordinance may be made at any time, adopted in any manner.
- The budget must appropriate *debt service*.
- *Contingency* may not exceed 5 percent of a fund.

All communities must have a *budget officer*. In communities with a manager form of government, the county or city manager is officially the budget officer. In other communities, other employees may be appointed the budget officer.

The *fiscal year* begins July 1 and ends June 30.

- Before *April 30* of each fiscal year each department head shall transmit budget requests to the budget officer.
- The budget, together with a budget message, must be submitted to the governing board not later than *June 1*.

The budget proposal, once presented to the governing body, must be made public.

- On the same day the budget is submitted to the governing body, the budget officer shall file a copy in the office of the clerk to remain available for *public inspection*.
- The budget shall be available to *news media*.
- A statement will be published that the budget has been submitted to the governing board and give notice of the time and place of the budget hearing.
- Before adopting the budget ordinance, the board shall hold a *public hearing*.

Property tax shall be levied sufficient to balance the budget. Property tax may not be adjusted mid-year (unless ordered by the Local Government Commission or a court).

Note: Key legal requirements and terms are excerpted from state statute. See G.S. 159-7 through -17.

Appendix B:
Revenue Sources and Authorized Spending Purposes of North Carolina Cities and Counties

Table 1. Major Revenue Sources Available to North Carolina Cities and Counties

Revenue Source	Available to Municipalities	Available to Counties
Local Taxes		
Property tax[†]	X	X
Local-option sales and use tax	‡	X
Privilege license taxes	X	X
Local Fees, Charges, and Assessments		
General user fees and charges	X	X
Regulatory fees	X	X
Public enterprise fees and charges	X	X
Franchise fees	X	X
Special assessments	X	X
State-Shared Revenue		
Video programming services taxes	X	X
Beer and wine taxes	X	X
Solid waste tipping tax	X	X
911 charge	X	X
Real estate transfer tax	X	X
Disposal taxes		X
Electric franchise tax	X	

(continued)

Table 1.   Major Revenue Sources Available to North Carolina Cities and Counties (*continued*)

Revenue Source	Available to Municipalities	Available to Counties
Telecommunications tax	X	
Piped natural gas tax	X	
Motor fuels tax (Powell Bill funds)	X	
Miscellaneous Revenue Sources		
Alcohol Beverage Control store profits	X	X
Investment earnings	X	X
Grants	X	X
Fines, penalties, and forfeitures	X	X
Minor revenue sources	X	X

Note: This list has been compiled from Kara A. Millonzi, *Local Government Revenue Sources in North Carolina* (Chapel Hill: UNC School of Government, 2011), which contains more detail on these revenue sources.

† For more detail on the rights and duties of local elected officials relating to the listing, assessment, levy, and collection of property taxes, see Christopher B. McLaughlin, *The Property Tax in North Carolina* (Chapel Hill: UNC School of Government, 2012).

‡ Counties are authorized to levy and share proceeds with municipalities.

Table 2. Authorized City versus County Spending Purposes

Service	Cities Authorized	Counties Authorized
Airports	X	X
Ambulance service	X	X
Animal shelters	X	X
Art galleries and museums	X	X
Auditoriums/coliseums	X	X
Building services	X	X
Buses/public transit	X	X
Cable television†		
Cemeteries	X	
Community appearance	X	X
Community colleges		X
Cooperative Extension		X
Court facilities (space only)	X	X
Economic development	X	X
Elections		X
Electric systems	X	
Emergency management	X	X
Environmental protection	X	X
Fire protection	X	X
Forest protection		X
Gas systems	X	
Historic preservation	X	X
Human relations	X	X
Jails	X	X
Job training	X	X
Juvenile detention homes		X
Law enforcement	X	X
Libraries	X	X
Mental health services		X
Parks and open space	X	X

(*continued*)

Table 2. Authorized City versus County Spending Purposes (*continued*)

Service	Cities Authorized	Counties Authorized
Planning and zoning	X	X
Public health services		X
Public housing	X	X
Public schools		X
Recreation programs	X	X
Register of deeds		X
Rescue squads	X	X
Sidewalks	X	
Social services		X
Soil and water conservation		X
Solid waste collection	X	X
Solid waste disposal (landfill)	X	X
Storm drainage	X	X
Street lighting	X	
Streets	X	
Traffic engineering	X	
Veterans services	X	X
Wastewater collection and treatment	X	X
Water supply and protection	X	X
Youth detention facilities		X

Note: North Carolina law grants cities and/or counties authority to provide the listed services (adapted from a list originally prepared by Catawba County). Throughout the state, the mix of services provided in any given county or municipality will vary.

† As of 2006, authorization for cable television franchises is permitted only by the state of North Carolina, but existing franchises may continue until their expiration.

Appendix C:
GFOA Guidelines on the Twelve Elements of the Budget Process

Establish Broad Goals to Guide Government Decision Making:

1. Assess community needs, priorities, challenges, and opportunities.
2. Identify opportunities and challenges for government services, capital assets, and management.
3. Develop and disseminate broad goals.

Develop Approaches to Achieve Goals:

4. Adopt financial policies.
5. Develop programmatic, operating, and capital policies and plans.
6. Develop programs and services that are consistent with policies and plans.
7. Develop management strategies.

Develop a Budget Consistent with Approaches to Achieve Goals:

8. Develop a process for preparing and adopting a budget.
9. Develop and evaluate financial options.
10. Make choices necessary to adopt a budget.

Evaluate Performance and Make Adjustments:

11. Monitor, measure, and evaluate performance.
12. Make adjustments as needed.

www.ingramcontent.com/pod-product-compliance
Lightning Source LLC
Chambersburg PA
CBHW080245270326
41926CB00020B/4378